THE POETRY OF MOHSEN NAMJOO

— BOOK 1 —

Angels and Demons

Translations by

Reza Arefi

Angels and Demons

©2022, Reza Arefi

Cover Art: Bahar Sabzevari (https://www.baharsabzevari.com)

publisher: wornoutsoles.com; contact: info@wornoutsoles.com.

ISBN: 978-1-66787-498-2

Translator's Note

Borges, that unmatchable maven of form, asserts there are only two legitimate ways of translating poetry: literal and recreation[1]. But unless it brings out the kind of strangeness that attains a certain beauty, he argues literal translation remains a paradox, therefore he permits the translators of his works to rephrase what he has done. The anonymous Japanese poet in Paterson[2] compares translating poems to taking a shower with a raincoat on, simply defeating the purpose. It is true that translating poems often becomes a futile effort, a kindergarten show-and-tell, a cry in the wind, a malfunctioning silencer in the eternal duel of form and content. But facing how form and content intertwine as they do in Mohsen Namjoo's poems, one embarks on a ship swaying in the sea of unexpected paradoxes. In his poems, form often becomes the dominant aspect of the content, and content often feeds the form. Words lose their encyclopedic meanings and morph like a chameleon into the background texture.

Each of Mohsen's poems is a journey—"can one be more cliché than this?"[3] Emerging from geopolitical necessities and personal transformations, his poems are not necessarily pleasing to the casual reader, nor do they appear as explicitly pensive to the implicit-minded. Yet translating them is always rewarding in the most uncommon and unexpected ways. In doing so, I inescapably traveled.

I went from the majestic coronation of the rhythm to the greasy ease of his street slang, sometimes in a single poem. Some poems are as intense as a volcano at the verge of eruption, some as simple as a chatty brook in early spring. In my attempts, I waded in the velvety grandiose of the clas-

1 *On Writing*, Jorge Luis Borges, 1972.
2 Paterson, movie by Jim Jarmusch, 2016.
3 A line from "This Entire Poem" included in this collection.

sical side of his tongue using obscure, yet beautiful, metrical patterns, but also slid on the sandpaper of the fiery words of a vulgar craftsman. At some times, I rhymed my way out of an overgrown forest of muse, and at others, I invented new words, as in "Verse", accepting all along that this effort could very well be a losing battle. The only solace I took was that I tried to maintain the dominant aspects of each poem: tone, air, rhythm, and vernacular. The stark differences in styles reflect those of the original poems.

In his poetry, Mohsen chooses a style in accordance with the content, ranging from classical metrical rhythms to blank verse to free verse. English poetry is an accentual syllabic verse, which uses qualitative meter, as opposed to the quantitative meter[4] used in Persian poetry, which is based on the length of syllables. As a result, finding the exact counterpart of the feet used in a Persian poem for its translation to English is impossible. However, in my view, in order to create some level of resemblance in mood and tonality, two aspects ought to be maintained in the translation: the length of the foot (e.g., two or three) and the number of feet in each line (e.g., tetrameter, pentameter, etc.). For instance, in the case of the poem "I Wonder," I chose the rarely used tetrameter amphibrach as the meter with the closest rhythm to that of the original poem, also a tetrameter with three-syllable feet.

Some of the poems contained in this small selection have been either partly or entirely used as lyrics for some of Mohsen's songs, for instance "Geopolitical Destiny" and "Neo-Kantian Views", which have remained quite popular over the years[5]. In translating these, I had the opportunity to also consider his musical performance and audio intonations as a third dimension adding depth to an otherwise flat form–content perspective. But overall, translating this selection benefitted enormously from discussing the context in detail directly with the poet, for which I am extremely grateful, in particular the aspects too personal to be readily gleaned from the original poems. Examples include "This Entire Poem," "Nothin," "Your Scent," and "I wonder."

In translating this selection of poems, at times I felt as if I am walking a third, thus illegitimate, path other than those endorsed by Borges, namely,

4 Quantitative meter is used in Persian poetry, as well as, for example, in ancient Greek and Sanskrit.
5 See Appendix for a complete list.

literal and recreation. Mohsen's poems are generally not categorized as visual due to his fascination with form and rhythm. If they were, I would have probably had no choice other than to recreate. But despite painting images being a rarity, his playful ways with words pull the reader's mind in different, often opposite, directions—"centrifugal, centripetal" as William Carlos Williams suggests[6]—thereby opening singular spaces that cannot be quickly filled with the next thought or image, as if leaving a lasting bas relief of amazement. It is for this reason that Borges's paradox could perhaps be avoided without the need to dismantle and dissect the poems through recreation. There was certainly no shortage of opportunities to create beautiful strangeness and stunning singularities by being literal. But to my delight, Mohsen's special playfulness with form allowed for the occasional reach to stain my brush with familiar hues on the palette of recreating context.

At the end, each poem became an affair in which I loved and lost. In some, I stayed faithful throughout, yet in others I cheated my way out.

Reza Arefi
September 2022

---

6 "The Poem", from *The Wedge*, William Carlos Williams, 1944.

Foreword
By Mohsen Namjoo

Let us suppose I can be considered a poet.

There are poets who died years before their translator. There are poets who are contemporary with their translator, but they have never met him. There are poets who have met their translator and are even close friends with him.

I suggest I am more fortunate than all those poets.

I doubt that aside from me there is any poet whose translator met him when he was a skinny, sloppy child of seven years old.

I am recounting this for the first time. I was fascinated by the pleasant appearance of one of my brother's friends who came to our house from time to time. His demeanor, his pale skin and impressive dark beard and mustache, made his face very much resemble the handsome military characters in the nineteenth-century Russian novels. Let me simply summarize this long description—when I was seven years old, Marcel Proust came to our door.

His name was Reza. Later, he and my brother moved to Tehran, and after that, when I was a teenager, I heard that he had moved out of Iran. Time passed and the clock struck forty thousand times,[7] until fate brought me, who by then had become a musician, to America for the first time in the summer of 2008. Six solo concerts were part of the tour. After the third concert, I felt that my energy was gradually running low, so I had to cut back on socializing after the concerts and rest enough to fly to the next city.

---

7 The expression is borrowed from the poem "Let's Believe in the Arrival of the Cold Season" by Iranian poet Forough Farrokhzad, 1934–1967.

When the Washington, D.C., performance was over, I wanted to leave the crowd as soon as possible and go to the hotel, when suddenly I saw a familiar face sitting in the corner of the big concert hall—Marcel Proust in America. Oh my God, after thirty years. More than thirty years.

I have been seeing him in America for years now, not a lot, maybe twice a year. After Corona, even less. Marcel Proust, in my mind, no longer has a mustache, but his heart is bigger than the original Proust, and I have no doubt that his knowledge of the Persian language, his native tongue, is much better than Proust's knowledge of his. And again, I have no doubt that Proust could never translate poems full of sounds and musical word games so well.

Without any exaggeration, I do not see any special features in my poems (if we consider them poems) that make them worthy of translation into another language. In fact, I think there is perhaps no feature in them that a non-Persian speaking reader would miss. Everything you see in this book is the result of Reza's hard work, Marcel Proust of my mind, and I have no role or credit in this regard. So, I thank him from the bottom of my heart and thank the readers for tolerating my words here. I kiss your hand.

Mohsen Namjoo
August 2022
Istanbul

Introduction
By Hamid Namjoo[8]

Mohsen Namjoo was born on March 6, 1976, in Torbat-e-Jaam in northeast Iran. He was the youngest child of a large traditional family. Despite Torbat-e-Jaam's fame for its folk dance and music, often performed in festivals throughout the world, performing and studying music was shunned in Mohsen's family due to strict religious beliefs. His enthusiastic interest in music became known in his preschool years but owning and learning how to play an instrument was forbidden for him. His persistence in following his interest led to obtaining permission from his parents for taking singing classes in the repertoire of Persian traditional music at the age of ten.

What is here referred to as Persian traditional music has a hundred-some year history even though it is sometimes claimed to be the continuation of mystical dance and music ("*samaa*") or the evolved version of the music played at the courts of Persian kings before Islam. However, during the period from around the time of the Safavids until the end of the Qajar dynasty, due to the expansion of the role Shiite religion played in all social and political aspects of the time, dirge and monody became the predominate forms of musical performance in Iran. It was only after the establishment of the constitutional monarchy in the early days of the twentieth century and the social and political changes it brought about that a few musicians familiar with Western classical music took on the task of collecting and classifying the remnants of old musical pieces, called "*radif*," which up to that point had survived only orally. The entire *radif* was classified into a modal system with

---

8 Hamid Namjoo is an Iranian writer and literary critic. He is the author of several novels and short story collections including *Spartacus* (Paris: Naakojaa, 2018). He is Mohsen's older brother.

xi

seven basic modes and four submodes, which now form the entire Persian traditional music repertoire.

A few years after training in vocal *radif*, Mohsen started to self-train himself with the Persian long-necked lute, or *"Seh-tar."* The intimate relation between Persian classical poetry and Persian traditional music motivated Mohsen to study poetry. In the coming years, he also paid specific attention to the folk music of northeast Iran and studied it with some of its masters. By the time he finished high school in 1995, he had already composed numerous traditional musical pieces accompanied by lyrics from classical poems. After finishing high school, he was accepted, with top national ranking, to Tehran University to study Persian traditional music.

In Tehran, Mohsen suddenly found himself in a dynamic environment, which allowed him to make strides into world literature, music, and theatre. In particular, he was further exposed to other genres of music including Western classical music, jazz, blues, rock, pop, and so on. This opened many windows in his mind and piqued his interest toward comparative studies of various genres—an interest that later led to his endeavors into new forms of music.

Living in a culturally quilted society that was, on the one hand, deeply under the influence of a fundamentalist take on religion and morality and, on the other hand, had a vibrant younger generation seeking a place in today's world through examining modern and postmodern philosophies, demolished all barriers around Mohsen's foundational beliefs. In addition, at Tehran University, he faced a very rigid academic environment in which traditional music was considered sacred and any change to its means of composition and performance was considered a grave sin. Facing closed doors anywhere he looked, he quit the university with the aim of independently working on his music, as if setting sail toward unknown waters in a handmade sailboat.[9]

Mohsen's first attempt was at liberating his music from the yoke of the Persian classical poetry, which has historically heavily influenced both rhythm and content. With over ten centuries of history, Persian classical

9 *Reflections on Namjoo, A Collection of Essays on the Music of Mohsen Namjoo* (UCI Jordan Center for Persian Studies, 2019), edited by Sahand Rahnama, pp. 109-127; article by Alireza Ehsani.

poetry reflects the evolution of thought in Iranian history. It would be more accurate to consider it not only poetry but rather a vehicle for conveying many aspects including philosophy, morality, aesthetics, and even mythology and history. Mohsen tried to give lyrics an identity independent from rhythm and melody. Meanwhile, he was well aware that poetry is an integral part of the traditional music, and instrumental pieces have limited audience. He thus handpicked poems that could be used outside the norm of those days. For instance, he chose words from classical poets such as Nasser Khosrow[10] and Roudaki[11] whose poems were not widely used, if at all, as lyrics for Persian traditional music due to their complex metrical feet, which did not easily lend themselves to the most common, simple rhythms used by traditional musicians.

His next attempt was to write lyrics of his own—lyrics emanated from the mind of a young poet in an extremely disparate society that would break the ancient norms in search for finding a path to the future. Parts of Mohsen's poetry is also influenced by the structures presented by Reza Baraheni[12] in "Addressing Butterflies." In Baraheni's world, poetry is an expression of an aesthetical mood. In his poetry, also referred to as linguistic poetry, tonality and rhythm are superior to content and meaning. To him, the poet is to remove all barriers between him and the words. The order in which words are placed, in spite of their meanings, is based on the mood and emotions of the poet—emotions that are a projection of the poet on his world and surroundings, perhaps a cry of desperation and pain. This way of phraseology goes beyond influencing the order of words and even affects its scansion. In other words, the analysis of the verse is also based on the intended and expressed rhythm.[13]

Many of Mohsen's poems, including some of the poems translated in this selection, have served as lyrics to his songs. It is therefore not surprising to find colloquial expressions in many of them. In Persian classical poetry, great care was always taken in choosing a formal literary vocabulary in line

10 Persian poet and writer of the eleventh century.
11 Persian poet of the tenth century.
12 Iranian novelist, poet, and literary critic, 1935–2022.
13 *Reflections on Namjoo, A Collection of Essays on the Music of Mohsen Namjoo* (UCI Jordan Center for Persian Studies, 2019), edited by Sahand Rahnama, pp. 27-29; article by Reza Baraheni.

with the often-profound content and often at the expense of verboseness. Even in the case of modern Persian poetry, in which the breakup of the metrical system and transition toward newer forms such as free verse became dominant, formal literary language still reigns, and use of colloquial terms have been infrequent. It is in Mohsen's poetry that we see the predominance of the use of a colloquial, and at times vulgar, language with, perhaps for the first time, tight integration with formal language in accordance with the content.

The ambiance of Mohsen's poems is an honest mirror to that of Iran after the 1979 Revolution. The breakdown of the social structure and excessive movement of its layers, major changes in social and moral values, and resistance of the social forces representing the old structure created a polarity and divergence in the society, which is all but present in Mohsen's work. On the one hand, the government and a large group of the population were romanticizing a return to traditional values, while on the other hand, maintaining the modern lifestyle built based on the most recent technological advancements from the West seemed inevitable. It is therefore not surprising to see that the ultimate goal in life for many of the younger generation has been to immigrate and leave behind the trauma of living in a bipolar society.

When he quit the university to free himself from the rigid academic environment, he soon realized that the situation outside was not any better. Access to funds and resources for making the kind of music not endorsed by the establishment was very difficult if not impossible. His music was not able to obtain necessary permissions for distribution. He observed firsthand that in the quilted society of the time, human values were mere mirages that quickly disappeared as clouds of hardship and devastation drifted in. Many of the diverging and multipolar aspects of the society he lived in are evident in his poems—melancholy, ruined hopes, broken hearts, social defeat and ever-present shadow of poverty and desolation. Perhaps it is the presence of these or similar themes, common in many regions, that has made Mohsen's works relatable by many of his generation in other parts of the world.

To bypass the government control, Mohsen eventually decided to forego the official permits and started sharing his music online, and as a result, quickly reached a new audience of hundreds of thousands. Yet he was threatened and persecuted in many ways until he finally left Iran in 2007.

Mohsen continues his investigations in poetry and music. In addition to several books, he has so far published eighteen albums, each one looking at music from a new and different vista point. His poetry is not necessarily supreme from an aesthetical point of view, something he does not pursue, but it is rebellious, keeps breaking the norms, and pushes the boundaries to new levels. His poems are an honest narration of the sufferings of his generation forgotten in the intersection of the old and the new.

Hamid Namjoo
August 2022

The good, the bad you behold in humans' mold

The joy, the sorrow you find in destiny foretold

Blame not the heavens, for in the realm of reason

Heavens more wretched than you a thousand fold

—*Omar Khayyam, Rubaiyat*

TABLE OF CONTENTS

Inevitably

Dusk;

    it is dusk, Sunday it must be.

Woman;

    staring at the scattered red, flirtatious has to be,

    disillusioned of another realm,

    washing away the fatigue of the day's masculine load she must be.

Dusk;

    fading into the night, dark necessarily.

Man;

    unveiling the ebony of the night, drunk he must be.

    will find the corpse of the morning in his repetitive bed,
    undoubtedly.

Dusk;

    inevitably glum

Night;

    inevitably lone

    inevitably tears

    inevitably cigarettes

Woman; Man;

    a love streaked over the skin of a day.

A day;

    inevitably cruel, inevitably bright,

    pregnant of a dusk and a night,

    red and dark,

    with no desire for coquetry and vice, inevitably.

Spring 1993

Verse

Akin to fire on lingering roads
My soul on chains, dreaming uproars.
Bearing no grudge, mind in denial
Silent in love I fall as I pass.

Indifferent and frail in flaring fatigues
I meander amongst drunkards en masse.
What for you busy your passionless head?
Never mind I say, I say as I pass.

***

Verse survives me.
The green back of a note survives me.
With blistery scientattlistic claws I die a halthearted tightoomphish death, and—
Death survives me.
Struction lives, deliraration lives, and we won't.
We die at the strashy hands of the nonsensical times.
Survives us word.
Survives us fod.
Survives us piss.
Cudful treasure of a rucksack survives us.
Recklessnestly buoyant birch-a-bra poem survives us.
And we sip survives us and we sip survives us.

And we sip the drip of the hardassdroolist.

We experience the shell of the usekisslerse.

Survives me verse.

Outlives me death.

"Vartan spoke not!

Sparkled for a moment in his torment, then leapt and left"[14]

—for Europe, seeking asylum.

Fall 1994 – Fall 2004

14 Liberal translation of a quote from the poem "Vartan's Death" by A. Shaumloo.

Stutter

Key in the ignition,

    Stutututututututututututter

    doesn't ignite the lamp you planted in my palm.

    Hey! You, the slumberous glyph of beige minarets.

In myself I impai…airfield[15] I am,

    so your blazing putt-putter crowlings[16]

    can land on my runway.

Key in the ignition,

    stutututututututututututter

    doesn't start, check here, check there, nothing at all,

    no matter how much of the hairy ambiance

                        I exert.

A maestro you wer…ay[17] back when

even stars   twirled your rosary   at street corners

in their blinky stinky lustful hands

        spinning,   staring,

        so they stare just like you at what

        you stare …

---

15 Morphing *impair* and *airfield*.
16 Young crows, in style of ducklings.
17 Morphing *were* and *way*.

No! No! Tell scrawny immortals whose lumb...are[18] odor remover of
your refrigerator:

Moldy are all the verses in there

—story of the brother's sold blood they reveal—

Say to them the black veil key and the return of the stick doesn't get
it stutututututututututututart.

No! Say! So they land on that runway of mine

so they become free...rebo...rneedfull...lovers[19].

Like the pink of these faces on which no strings

for the smeared hairy caress of no mother-fucker flag-bearer can
be tuned.

Say! Say that came all those like you and Moses
and Jesususususususususustutter

as much did we,

didn't fucking start.

Spring 1996

18 Morphing *lumbar* and *are*.
19 Morphing *free*, *reborn*, *needful*, and *lovers*.

Your Scent

This you spread your scent this very scent you spread that I know
not the name of on every street that spread you do your scent

{a hundred years passed on my flesh and a hundred tasteless houses
depart from you would—

that spread you do your scent on every street}

{still after a hundred years and my lingering limbs stuck in between
the rock and a foolish hard place

that wreaks of sorrow, as open my eyes you would—

that spread you do your scent on every street}

{when after a hundred years the rock turns into confetti in my hands
and you run, you come, you chill out you would—

that spread you do your scent on every street}

{just if you knew the rock is the sea and I the shipwrecked you faint
and die you would—

that spread you do your scent on every street}

{a hundred years passed on the flesh of this gullible me whose chest is
hoarse from the cold of being by you put off you would—

that spread you do your scent on every street}

{madly with your hand-laden scent as you lay your head on my pillow every night as if my head under hydraulic press you press you would—

that spread you do your scent on every street}

Spread as you do the name on every street …

Fall 1996

Faint Flames in the Rosarium

You resemble these very flames

       … lames … ames

I uttered already.

You resemble these very flames

       … lames … ames

and I, your cold ash

       smashaplash!

You resemble these very flames

lone, yet warm and pleasant

with no resolve left to burn.

You resemble these very flames and I reveal

you are the rosarium who turned me into Abraham

    the rosarium that turned me into Abraham

    for I have become Abraham, The Rosarium[20].

I walk on you,

       … lames … ames

I walk on,

       … lames … ames

No longer will I break your heart on rocks

       … lames … ames

20 A reference to Ebrahim Golestan, Iranian artist. Golestan is rosarium in Persian and Ebrahim is the Persian pronunciation of Abraham. The poem refers to the biblical story of the young Abraham in which, upon breaking idols, he was ordered to walk over fire. The fire did not burn him, for it turned into roses.

I walk on.

You are the flames of this unclaimed love.

How knightly you dress in that resolute mural of yours,

for you are the resolute rosarium maybe and I, its Abraham.

Winter 1996

This Entire Poem[21]

This entire poem,

of which I have not written more than three words yet,

which have not written before yet,

wants to say the air

is not enough to live on

and light is needed, too.

And this implies

if the poem is explicit

the poet could be dead

could be blind,

in full.

And this implies the one who explicates

is in love,

who could be blind

and dead.

So, deprive him of air, but

        not of your laughs.

21 The recurring theme in this poem, translated here as "deprive me of …/not of your …", is taken
from the poem "Tu Risa" by Pablo Neruda, which opens with:

Quítame el pan, si quieres,	*Take bread away from me, if you wish*
quítame el aire, pero	*Take air away, but*
no me quites tu risa.	*Do not take from me your laughter.*

From: *The Poetry of Pablo Neruda*, edited by Ilan Stavans, 2005.

Deprive him of air, but

        not of your tears,

for a single hidden stinky hair of yours is above and beyond my
purchasing power.

I am one of those eighty-page single-space notebooks I bind everyday.
you are the beautiful breath
of my unhealed soul.

You are the sun—
can one be more cliché than this? —
Well, you are the sparkle.
No, you are that same sun,
who has not stayed, does not, will not behind the clouds
stay no more.
Many thirty years passes before
I will be healed again,
if you wish.
And you,
hey, you!
Unhealed me and I hail you.

So, deprive me of air,

        not of your laughs.

Deprive me of air, of space,
of food, of fate, of pleasures,

        not of your laughs.

Deprive me of light,

        not of your flames.

Deprive me of vows,

not of your tears.

I am naked and baked of your ways,

might be dead, I even think

        but … not of your laughs.

Improbable I am being alive.

Blessed be the hand ripping my groin apart.

I am the most recent of deaths in the series of your kills[22].

I am the mate of your meals.

Deprive me of food and means,

        not of your garden of laughter.

Have killed me your lips and teeth,

and all those limbs grown on your core,

        but … not of your laughs.

Have killed me, have hidden my corpse.

And all I know is you the remover of the mirrors,

you the queen of the mirrors,

you who gaze into the mirrors

for which my corpse is hidden from your gaze,

blood-red tulips have grown from my corpse.

I have been killed and thrown under the tulip petals of your

earlobe,

that same earlobe,

---

22 Original poem includes a reference to a series of political assassinations in Iran in the 90s.

that same crescent of the petals of your earlobe,

the beginning bang of the entire universe.

Deprive me of the universe,

of sanctums,

of autumns,

of blowing winds.

O blowing winds! Throw me off this tower of mine,

so crashes this poet of all these lines,

so falls this dead man of residing under the petals.

Many a thirty years, many a forty years passes since

this poet is hiding under there.

Deprive him of air,

of blowing air,

of howling winds,

of me, of he, who is the one who writes no original lines.

I am a cliché.

I am those eighty-page notebooks of single lines,

two lines,

and tens of lines if I even write

cannot be freed this love of mine.

Love is filling a matchbox with twenty-thousand sunflower
seeds.

Love is hanging on to each other's needs

when the entire world is adrift,

is left alone,

and freed.

Deprive me of freedom,

        not of your laughs,

of stumbles,

        not of your tears,

of devotion, of delight, … no, my desired!

Of my destitute,

        not of your ire,

of des … no!

… ur ire … no!

des …

… ire

Dés…

…irée[23]

This entire poem before I write it,

meant to say just this.

Fall 1997

---

23 In the final lines of this poem, words and letters are gradually tossed away to reveal the name of the poet's lover, which has a literal translation of *desire*, or *desired*, closest to which is the French name Désirée.

Two Lands

Two lands;   One a country, the other one, too.

Two lands;   One, America 2/4, the other, Iran 6/8.

Two lands;   In this world.

Two lands, not! Two worlds.

From the speed up of this to the sarcasm of the other,

From a handgun in this to the birds of the prairies in the other,

From this side of the twenty-first to the other side of the
eighth century.

I, who got lost in the mystics' maze,

I, who is the brainchild of laze,

I, who aimed high always.

Here, a corpse and degradation:

Neither do I fit here,

Nor am I accepted there.

Here, some form of death and inspiration:

Neither do I dissolve here,

Nor am I welcomed there.

Certainly won't pass even as a lowly singer of blues or jazz.

Two illusory lands hanging from the impossible.

Anything, everything implausible.

Turn right.

Turn left.

No! Go straight[24].

Fall 2000

---

24 Final three lines of the original poem are in English.

Golden Egg

One day your chicken too will lay a golden egg.
You sell the golden egg, you buy a life instead.
There is a place still with skies the color blue,
Seas the greenest of greens ... folks the greenest of greens.

One day your chicken too will put on makeup.
You put a kiss on that face, you live a life instead.
There are folks still who put on black makeup,
Cocoa by color ... cocoa by taste.

One day you lay a double-yolk egg just like your chicken.
You slay yourself daft for your chicken, you split your heart
in half for your chicken.
There is a mirage still that turns to water as you arrive,
With true jubilation ... real deeeeeep exhilaration.

One day all chickens will make fois gras.
You devour that fois gras, spread with basil over Melba.
There are words still to make your heart sink,
Eyes filled with tears of joy ... cheeks wet from tears of joy.

One day the chicken of your soul will pluck all its feathers,
You toss the feathers inside a pillow, you rest your head
outside the pillow.
There's around still a reason in this world,
Worthy of all your tears … worthy of all your laughs.

Summer 2001

Lolita

Once I knew of a Lolita
    still-life artisan
        pampered in plush,
            Tehran.

And Ahmad,
    a high school grad
        displeased driver of a yellow cab,
            Mashad.

Both from the time of the sudden loss
of everything on every side,
Iran.

Ahmad said:
"O, Lolita! I am the weary cavalry
of destiny
whose generation's dreams
all withered,"
and Lolita fell in love with that withered,
    in love with that Ahmad
        the wilted cavalry on his yellow sickly stead,
           his cab.

***

Twenty-five years passed.

    I know of a Lolita

        who I don't know much about,

           Tehran.

And I, a displeased high school grad

no license, no horse, not a sickly mule even,

nowhere across this land.

The grand halogen floodlight of hope

flickers in me.

Not enough of a fool, not enough of a cheat I am

    to brazenly claim

        "I am the weary cavalry

           of destiny."

Neither my generation has dreams whatsoever to lose

nor have I means to flee

or the will to move my lazy ass

or to end this life.

Hence no Lolita would keep me,

not even in her recycle bin.

I let go and move on

    jolly and glum

        ass lazy

           heart bruised.

Spring 2002

Speaker Cord

I have it better than the rest of the world.
Enough said that I am the speaker cord.
Stamped upon for sure, but I'm not dropping the sword.

I am nothing but an instrument
connecting the speaker end toward
that other, creating the lovely chord,
for I am the speaker cord.

Seemingly never I was alone left,
for the idle times by your side I wasn't on my own left—

                              felt right forevermore.

On Love I rode then.
Skin on yours I erode then.
My life to you I owed then.
Threw in my abode then,
the moments our wings in the wind we billowed then,
the moments we filled the space in between our every
node then,
the moment I with you released my load then.

How did I turn? O' my adored,

how was it then? I did stay aboard,

I stayed all aboard.

How do I word?

How do I wor...m-screw[25] ... and afterlife ... ay yayay yayay...

For I am a sucker of a speaker cord.

Summer 2002

---

25 Morphing *word* and *worm-screw*.

Anywhere in the World We

Anywhere in the world we reached for was slippery, toilsome to climb!

No breadcrumbs ever crossed our plates.

No revelations were ever brought to light.

Gone with the wind blown on everything prior had wreaked

the wind of wreck.

Anything we touched, tremors of a beaten corpse.

How many times we were frightened, how many?

How many times we became the bee sting of a childhood?

How many times we groaned as if our hearts cried?

Why does the leprechaun of pain always visit us?

Summer 2002

Geopolitical Destiny

One day you will wake up
Figure you've lost it all
No friends left around you
You've forgotten them all
A few more white hair
On your flimsy skull
Your birthday party yet
Another funeral
You've totally given up on all
Your back humped even more this year
Your shoulders lower than the prior
Look closely around you
See the indiscriminate fire
This being born in Asia
Is your geopol destiny
Your life's up in the air
Your breakfast, just a smoke with tea

Hey! You almighty of the heavens
Tell me for God's sake
What's on that mind of yours
When do *we* get a break?

That you get told to put hands on your head

That for them you're as good as dead

That they don't let you in on their game

That they take you as a joke so lame

This being born in Asia

Is your geopol destiny

Your life's up in the air

Your breakfast, just a smoke with tea

Winter 2002

Miniscript

Lay not your hand on me.

At your hand I am filled with misery.

Your awful acts are fresh still beneath my memory.

Spare me do your dear flesh, liberate me of your cunning grit.

Embrace thee I will never for a century commit.

Keep your hands off me!

Off! Off! Keep your hands off me!

Winter 2002

Nothin

All is left to the Creator's will
inside the pious-minded jail.
Down a lonely darkening pit
nostalgic depths of blues prevail.
The grief for the dead, a colorful veil.

You dump me and go, you leave me alone.
Got the urge to show off then put off this moan.

Know enough I do to know I am naught.
You sure nuff ain't know nothin, dude.

Flashing a sergeant's badge,
sorrow, an unbearable beast.
Rejoice at pay raise as much you can feast.

"For He is one, and none there is but Him."
So cuz He ain't there, then there ain't nothin.

2002

Deceit

You, the street sweeper at dawn of love,

You, the all, the everything of love,

I, a bottom stone of a wheat mill.

You, tea leaves tale of your ancient kin.

O love! Deceived me before you withdrew.

The novice quick juggler! My house on

fire you set and fled. You shot away

Arash-like[26] an arrow before you flew.

You, the blue crystal talk of the town.

You, a pristine cupful of Danube.

You, the pleated bashful skirt of chaste.

You, from south to north in your embrace.

O love!

Heads, one by one, rolling in the trenches,

With my guilty blood filled up to the brim.

My five hundred armies at your service.

The masses, every single one, contrite.

---

26 A symbol of sacrifice, Arash is a famous bowman in Persian mythology who, upon occupation of
the country by enemy forces, accepted their demeaning challenge to mark the new border with the
flight of his arrow. His arrow, fed by his own life, flew for several days and landed where the border
had been prior to the occupation.

You, the Bach of a meek in the heart.

You, the Damavand[27] of a sigh to a hill.

You, the closer-to-me-than-my-veins flute.

You, the sunk-as-wail-in-my-heart fiddle.

2002

---

27 Highest peak in Iran. More than eighteen thousand feet, Mt. Damavand is the highest volcano in Asia. According to mythology, Arash climbed Mt. Damavand to shoot his arrow.

Neo-Kantian views

Neo-Kantian views belong to me,

Les fleurs de Normandie sont pour vous.

Charms and haste are my share,

Six-inch love affairs are for you.

Cool, yet brainy, belongs to us,

Tamarind maccheroni belongs to us,

Avenue de Martyr Candy belongs to us,

The grave to parody belongs to us.

Neo-Kantian views belong to me;

Les fleurs de Normandie sont pour vous.

Where do you park your pony, gringo?

What do you mock, you phony jingo?

You're hanging by a thread, Sir, Your Honor.

What'd you stand for, Ma'am, You're a goner.

Neo-Kantian views belong to me;

Les fleurs de Normandie sont pour vous.

Why throw a feast, you insatiable beast?

What vespers you whisper, *my man de la fin?*

Why do you keep searching, you wailing creed?

You've really got balls, my dear lead.

Bootleg copy of *The Godfather* belongs to us.

Stale patties for the supper, too.

Uninvited creation is certainly us.

An embarrassed administrator, too.

"Maybe tomorrow!" is worthily ours.

Losing national team players, too.

Thickness of the dossiers is markedly ours.

Constructive criticism manners, too.

But *maybe* tomorrow belongs to us.

Maybe tomorrow belongs to us.

Eff my Neo-Kantian points of view;

    Tout vous le souhaitez sont pour vous.

Winter 2003

Octothorpe-Ass

Give a beetle a nudge

turns into an octothorpe-ass

many a horn flung out suddenly on every side.

Knows not, little miserable thing, which side of his I pass.

My little pinky to him, a bulldozer alright.

Given me a nudge the world,

horns I have suddenly flung out many a time,

paced this alien land to and fro,

brimming with a pride slinging even the earth out of its orbit.

But I, a miserable in the know,

misery, all I know;

this very earth, the little pinky of the world.

yet surprise, for I have suffered

despite my flung-out horns.

Fall 2004

Stink of Jasmines

Awash is the alley in stink of narcissi.

Gaze at the sunrays, if got nothin to do,

if got goo, flu, spew, no clue!

Blind if you wish to become, gaze at the sunrays.

You flatter me!

You blabber, it's phlegm you jabber!

Sell out not to the shadows, praise not the potent!

Mare's soul fled the scene, rebel soul flows serene.

Awash is the alley in stink of narcissi;

Gaze at pleasures of the days passing by!

Get stuck in traffic jam for a little while

to enjoy daylight.

       Ha! It's nighttime.

Screw a little to relax at nighttime.

       Ha! It's daylight.

Ha! It's nighttime.   Ha! It's daylight.

Ha! It's nighttime.   Ha! It's daylight.

Ha! It's nighttime.   Ha! It's daylight.

Ha! It's nighttime.   Ha! It's daylight.

Ha! It's nighttime.   Ha! It's daylight.

Ha! It's nighttime.   Ha! It's daylight.

Ha! Fuck it! You kicked the bucket!

Ha! You got shafted! Instead, had a hell of a time!

Hell of a time!

time.

time.

time.

Awash is the alley in stink of jasmines, in stink of narcissi.

Winter 2005

Alas

Enraged, pallid beliefs are dormant
Inert partial notions on my mind.
Conflict of heart and mind, pure folly
Discord of beasts and heavens, I find.

Rigid, absolute views, why to bear?
Falsified truths, I would never dare.
The soothing shrink, a great listener
His patchwork dogmas, but grave shortfall.

Alas! The teary feel of self-dejection.
Alas! The imploding feel of a downfall.

To whole from parts one cannot attain
Yet shallow brash parts I cannot refrain.

Oh man! Oh man! Slay utopian reveries.
Excrete on your adored, become the monodies.

Winter 2017

I Wonder …

I wonder if death is upon me reposing,
Quixote[28] within me to come to discerning
To not be the righteous maternal descendent,
The carnal affection to falter, demising.

The alternate notes of nightmarish lamenting,
I wonder, are tremolo plucking of mankind,
Illusions prevailing; extinction's ignoring
The Valley Neander[29]—A Heavenly blunder.

I wonder at holding the death in my bosom
If ever I see revelations approaching,
The wretched quintessence of dust[30] to repine on
The greasy unease of the open enigma.

My body was neither reacting to action,
My lazy demeanor was nor to attraction.
I haven't examined the mass of the cosmos
Because of the loony Supreme of the masses.

28 Reference to Don Quixote's idealistic delusions.
29 The Neander Valley in western Germany is where one of the first specimens of Homo Neander-thalensis were found.
30 Reference to Hamlet, Act 2, Scene 2, "What a piece of work is a man! … And yet, to me, what is this quintessence of dust?"

Or I if weren't at the bottom bemoaning

Or even elated, or even at all in,

A thousand lament of the woodwinds unable

To ravage my every inertial minutia.

I wonder the gracious embrace of the passing,

Is clothing the cloak of the softest of satins

With pleasing acoustic sensational caress

Announcing to Mohsen: Rejoice in the silence[31].

Fall 2018

---

31 Reference to Hamlet's final words, Act 5, Scene 2, "The rest is silence."

Angels and Demons

                  Angels and demons I give …

Black bile of fall and descension

Is what's gushing out of my every cell.

Down a cowardly hell.

Goings grouchy, unwell.

Hundred faces of dejection

Are twirling in my sucker of a DNA.

Test results TBA.

Ouch! … are TBA.

                  Angels and demons I give …

Total suspect's my healing.

Out of tune is my pleading.

Melancholy is to vainly cross

From my east to my west is bleeding.

Ouch! 'Tis suspect!

Ouch! No respect!

The lonely land's a disaster.

The very top of the raster.

And everyone's a blaster.

Directly down from the master.

Ah, my flesh peeling away,

A leprotic mange on display,

Blending in with decay.

Under the weight of a Godly Trust[32]

I'm crushed and pooped out and squashed.

Ah! I'm all destroyed.

Ouch! Achingly bored.

Affairs, total discord.

          Angels and demons I give … no fuck!

Winter 2019

---

32 Referring to the concept of the "Trust" presented by God to man after heaven and earth refused to accept.

Appendix

List of poems in this selection which have been used fully, or partially, as lyrics to Mohsen Namjoo's songs (See https://www.mohsennamjoo.com/):